LOOKING AT THE HUMAN IMPACT ON THE ENVIRONMENT WITH GRAPHIC ORGANIZERS

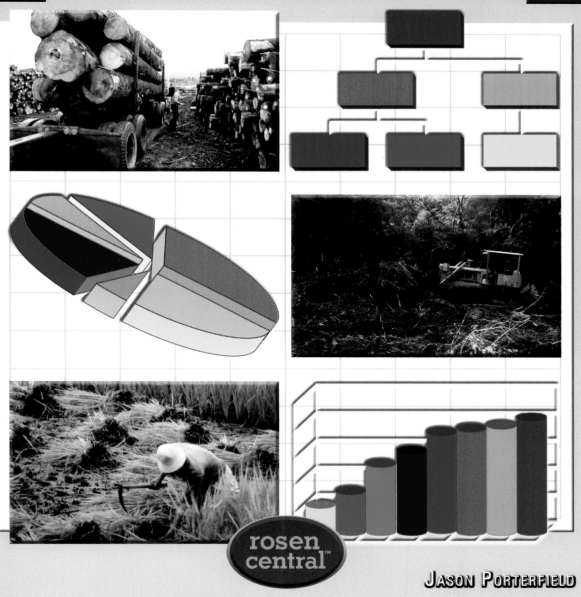

rosen
central™

JASON PORTERFIELD

The Rosen Publishing Group, Inc., New York

Published in 2006 by The Rosen Publishing Group, Inc.
29 East 21st Street, New York, NY 10010

Library of Congress Cataloging-in-Publication Data

Porterfield, Jason.
Looking at the human impact on the environment with graphic organizers/
Jason Porterfield.—1st ed.
   p. cm.—(Using graphic organizers to study the living environment)
Includes bibliographical references.
ISBN 1-4042-0614-0 (lib. bdg.)
1. Human ecology—Graphic methods. 2. Nature—Effect of human beings
on—Graphic methods. 3. Environmental impact analysis—Graphic methods.
I. Title. II. Series.
GF23.G7P67 2006
304.2--dc22

2005022040

Manufactured in the United States of America

On the cover: A bar chart *(top right)*, a pie chart *(center)*, and a tree chart *(bottom left)*.

CONTENTS

INTRODUCTION

Human beings have been Earth's dominant species for many thousands of years. Over time, the planet has undergone many changes, from ice ages to shifting continents. Humans have changed Earth's environment in small ways since the first fish was caught and the first garden was tended. Throughout much of history, these changes have been local and have had little effect on the rest of the world. However, the past 300 years have seen major technological innovations and changes in the way people exploit resources.

These changes are reflected in the recent environmental problems that concern many scientists, environmentalists, and governments around the world. People have released pollutants and greenhouse gases into the atmosphere, contributing to a global warming phenomenon. To meet the growing population's demand for food, more of Earth's surface is being used as farmland than ever before. Forests, wetlands, and arid regions are modified or eliminated

The scope of the human impact on the environment increases as humans advance technologically. Four examples of human activities that affect the environment are logging *(left)*, oil drilling *(top right)*, swamp-draining *(middle right)*, and mining *(bottom right)*.

to create this new farmland. More of the world's streams and rivers are dammed to meet the demand for water, while natural reservoirs of freshwater are becoming depleted. Many of these changes affect other life-forms, sometimes resulting in species extinctions. If the rate of global change does not slow, many species will disappear along with the world's dwindling resources.

The human impact on the environment can be shown using graphic organizers, tools used to present information in a way that is easy to understand. Graphic organizers come in many different forms, including graphs, tables, maps, and charts. They can serve as a useful means to demonstrate the extent of the human impact on Earth and what it means for the future.

CHAPTER ONE

THE ATMOSPHERE

The atmosphere is the enormous envelope of gases that surrounds Earth and enables it to sustain life. It traps energy from the sun as well as heat radiating from Earth itself. All life on Earth is dependent on the atmosphere for breathable gases. Oxygen, which is breathed by humans and animals, makes up about one-fifth of the atmosphere.

The atmosphere is so expansive that for many decades it seemed human activity could do little to affect it. Factories and people in cities polluted the air without considering the consequences. However, as the human population has grown and its needs have evolved, people have begun to realize that human

T-CHART: LAYERS OF THE ATMOSPHERE

LAYER	ALTITUDE ABOVE SEA LEVEL
EXOSPHERE	400 TO ABOUT 6,000 MILES (644 TO 9,660 KM)
THERMOSPHERE	50 TO 400 MILES (80 TO 644 KM)
MESOSPHERE	30 TO 50 MILES (48 TO 80 KM)
STRATOSPHERE	10 TO 30 MILES (16 TO 48 KM)
TROPOSHERE	SEA LEVEL TO 10 MILES (16 KM)

A T-chart is a simple two-column table useful for giving one layer of information, such as a definition, for a list of related concepts. This T-chart outlines the parameters of the five layers of the atmosphere.

activity can alter the atmosphere and, as a result, impact human well-being. Air pollution has been linked to health problems such as asthma and some forms of cancer.

Acid rain is one of the more notorious consequences of air pollution. When fossil fuels such as coal and oil are burned, they produce sulfur and nitrogen compounds as waste. These compounds bind with water vapor and fall to Earth's surface as a haze or in rain form. They can change the composition of bodies of water in a process called acidification. Areas of North America and Europe with naturally acidic soil are sometimes incapable of supporting life after acidification. Acid precipitation also corrodes buildings, reduces forest productivity, and may damage human health.

Air pollutants reduce air quality in urban and high-altitude areas. Smog is a type of heavy air pollution composed of particles from burning fossil fuels and evaporated chemicals from petroleum-based substances such as paints and gasoline. Ozone is a naturally occurring gas in the upper atmosphere, but it is a harmful air pollutant. It is produced by industrial emissions, automobile exhaust, and chemical solvents reacting to light in the atmosphere. Ozone can irritate the respiratory system and trigger asthma attacks.

TRACE GASES AND GLOBAL WARMING

The process by which the atmosphere traps energy from the sun is called the greenhouse effect. The atmosphere maintains an important balance between the amount of energy it traps and the amount of energy it releases. This delicate balance is dependent on the composition of the atmosphere.

Water vapor is the gas primarily responsible for the greenhouse effect on Earth. Because water vapor cools to become a solid or liquid at relatively low temperatures, the vapor returns to Earth as precipitation, preventing a buildup of water vapor in the atmosphere. Some of the sun's energy is, therefore, allowed to leave Earth's atmosphere. This process helps maintain moderate temperatures capable of sustaining life.

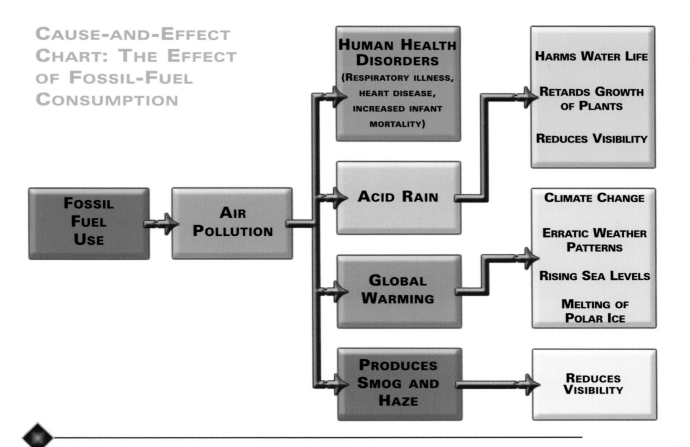

CAUSE-AND-EFFECT CHART: THE EFFECT OF FOSSIL-FUEL CONSUMPTION

FOSSIL FUEL USE	→	AIR POLLUTION	→	HUMAN HEALTH DISORDERS (RESPIRATORY ILLNESS, HEART DISEASE, INCREASED INFANT MORTALITY)	→	HARMS WATER LIFE / RETARDS GROWTH OF PLANTS / REDUCES VISIBILITY
				ACID RAIN		
				GLOBAL WARMING	→	CLIMATE CHANGE / ERRATIC WEATHER PATTERNS / RISING SEA LEVELS / MELTING OF POLAR ICE
				PRODUCES SMOG AND HAZE	→	REDUCES VISIBILITY

This cause-and-effect chart shows a chain of events that results from a single root cause; in this instance, fossil-fuel use. Cause-and-effect charts are flexible enough to show many types of causal relationships.

Many scientists studying the atmosphere believe that ever-increasing amounts of certain trace gases are contributing to global warming. Global warming is a general warming of Earth's temperature. During this ongoing process, excess greenhouse gases trap heat from the sun and Earth's own core without allowing the excess heat to radiate away from Earth. Human activity, particularly over the past 300 years, is seen as the primary cause of the increase in greenhouse gases.

Carbon dioxide is the greenhouse gas most frequently blamed as a cause of global warming. Carbon dioxide occurs naturally in the atmosphere, making up about 0.035 percent of atmospheric gases, or 350 parts per milliliter by volume (ppmv). It cycles through nearly

Among other effects, smog reduces visibility. This photograph, taken on September 29, 1966, shows how smog obscures the view of a section of San Francisco, California, from the San Francisco–Oakland Bay Bridge.

all living things in some form. Humans and other animals breathe in oxygen and exhale carbon dioxide as a waste, releasing it into the atmosphere. There, plants take it in and use the carbon to produce nutrients through a process known as photosynthesis, producing oxygen as a waste. This exchange of gases, known as the carbon cycle, is necessary for the survival of both plants and animals.

Under natural circumstances, the carbon cycle maintains a balance of oxygen and carbon dioxide in the atmosphere. However, since the Industrial Revolution began in the eighteenth century, people have been producing increasing amounts of carbon dioxide as a side effect of industry and urban growth. By analyzing air bubbles trapped in glacial ice, scientists can estimate the atmosphere's carbon dioxide levels throughout history. The carbon dioxide level may have been as low as 260 ppmv prior to the Industrial Revolution. Concentrations in the atmosphere have increased by as much as 25 percent since the eighteenth century.

The combustion of fossil fuels for manufacturing, generating electricity, and transportation is the major source of the increase of carbon dioxide in the atmosphere. Other human activities, especially deforestation, contribute to this increase. Millions of acres of woodland are destroyed every year to meet human needs. When large swaths of forest are removed from the carbon cycle, it becomes impossible for remaining trees to balance the excess carbon dioxide. Moreover, trees release carbon dioxide into the atmosphere after they are cut down, either when they are burned or as they decay.

CLUSTER CHART: SOURCES OF GREENHOUSE GASES

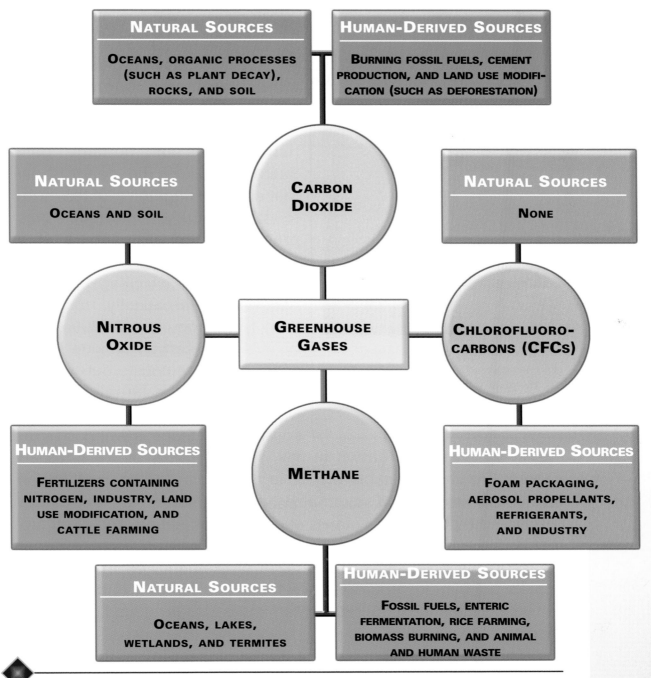

NATURAL SOURCES

OCEANS, ORGANIC PROCESSES (SUCH AS PLANT DECAY), ROCKS, AND SOIL

HUMAN-DERIVED SOURCES

BURNING FOSSIL FUELS, CEMENT PRODUCTION, AND LAND USE MODIFICATION (SUCH AS DEFORESTATION)

CARBON DIOXIDE

NATURAL SOURCES

OCEANS AND SOIL

NATURAL SOURCES

NONE

GREENHOUSE GASES

NITROUS OXIDE

CHLOROFLUORO-CARBONS (CFCs)

HUMAN-DERIVED SOURCES

FERTILIZERS CONTAINING NITROGEN, INDUSTRY, LAND USE MODIFICATION, AND CATTLE FARMING

METHANE

HUMAN-DERIVED SOURCES

FOAM PACKAGING, AEROSOL PROPELLANTS, REFRIGERANTS, AND INDUSTRY

NATURAL SOURCES

OCEANS, LAKES, WETLANDS, AND TERMITES

HUMAN-DERIVED SOURCES

FOSSIL FUELS, ENTERIC FERMENTATION, RICE FARMING, BIOMASS BURNING, AND ANIMAL AND HUMAN WASTE

This graphic organizer is called a cluster chart, which is useful for presenting relationships between concepts, events, or things. The main idea goes at the center of the chart, and the related concepts are clustered around it, sometimes in several levels. This cluster chart has two layers of information about greenhouse gases: the four types (in circles around the center rectangle) and their natural and human-derived sources (the rectangles that branch off from the circles).

Most power plants release dangerous pollutants into the air through smokestacks, and empty chemical wastes into nearby bodies of water.

Other trace gases in the atmosphere also contribute to the greenhouse effect. Scientists are particularly concerned about rising levels of methane gas. Examinations of ice cores show that until the beginning of the eighteenth century, methane was present in the atmosphere at a stable level, around 600 parts per billion by volume (ppbv). This level has risen dramatically, to more than 1,700 ppbv in the 1990s.

As with carbon dioxide in the atmosphere, scientists believe that human activity is largely responsible for this increase. One major source of methane is wet rice farming, in which rice is grown in still, shallow pools of water called paddies. As the vegetable matter in the pools decays, methane is released. Livestock cultivation also produces methane. Plant matter consumed by domestic animals such as cows, sheep, and oxen ferments in the animals' stomachs before it is digested, a process that results in the production and release of methane. As the growing human population requires more food, rice farming and livestock cultivation continue to increase. Methane is also produced during the burning of fossil fuels.

Though the present level of methane is far lower than that of carbon dioxide, scientists are concerned about the rapid increase. Both carbon dioxide and methane have a high infrared absorption band in their spectrums, meaning that they are capable of absorbing a high amount of energy from the sun. An increase in methane alone probably would not have a huge impact on the health of the atmosphere, since it is present in such small amounts. However,

INCREASED RISK OF SKIN CANCER AND CATARACTS

OZONE DEPLETION ALLOWS MORE UV RADIATION INTO THE ATMOSPHERE

DESTRUCTION OF PLANKTON POPULATIONS IN THE OCEANS

DAMAGE TO CROPS THAT DEPEND ON CERTAIN UV-SENSITIVE BACTERIA TO RETAIN NITROGEN

An e-chart is a simple tree diagram roughly in the shape of the letter *E*. It can be used to present a wide range of relationships between a main idea and supporting details. The main idea goes on the left, and the supporting details—in this instance, the effects of ozone depletion—go on the branches of the *E* on the right.

the levels of other trace gases, such as nitrous oxide and chlorofluorocarbons, are also increasing.

Nitrous oxide enters the atmosphere through deforestation, burning fossil fuels, and the use of nitrogen-based fertilizers. Chlorofluorocarbons, or CFCs, are used in refrigeration, fire extinguishers, and aerosol cans. They are very effective at absorbing and trapping heat even at very small levels, but CFCs are usually associated with the depletion of the ozone layer, a portion of the stratosphere that protects Earth from harmful ultraviolet (UV) radiation from the sun. The discovery of a hole in the ozone layer over Antarctica in 1985 confirmed scientists' theories that CFCs could negatively impact the ozone layer. Though the hole fluctuates in size, it was recently measured as being larger in area than North America.

Global warming is a controversial topic. Many scientists believe that the rise in greenhouse gas levels are contributing to a global warming trend, in which Earth's temperature rises, affecting everything from water levels to massive species extinctions. Others hypothesize that the global warming trend will eventually result in colder weather and perhaps another ice age. An ever-decreasing minority of scientists refuses to believe that global warming exists at all.

CHAPTER TWO

SHAPING THE LAND

Much of Earth's land surface is too cold, wet, dry, or rugged for large-scale settlements. However, the world's population is constantly growing and people are continually devising new ways to make use of Earth's resources. Even some of the most remote and uninhabitable areas are now affected by human activity.

Humans use the land for two primary purposes: settlement and cultivation. Human activity impacts land covers, such as grasslands, forests, and wetlands, in two ways. Conversion is the act of changing the land cover from one type to another. People clear forests to make pasture lands or drain swamps to cultivate crops. Eventually, croplands are converted into settlements as urban areas expand.

The second type of change is modification, in which existing land cover is altered but not transformed. Land cover is usually modified to increase its productivity. Forests are thinned to allow other trees to grow for future harvesting, fields are fertilized and irrigated in order to boost crop production, and infrastructure in urban areas, such as roads and utilities, is constantly repaired and redeveloped.

The most drastic changes to land use and land covers occur during periods of frontier expansion, when humans begin entering and changing pristine land. In the United States, the most active frontier period took place between 1862 and 1900, when the vast prairies of the American Midwest were converted from open grasslands to farms. The spread of humanity over the

PIE CHART: THE DECLINE OF U.S. FOREST LAND

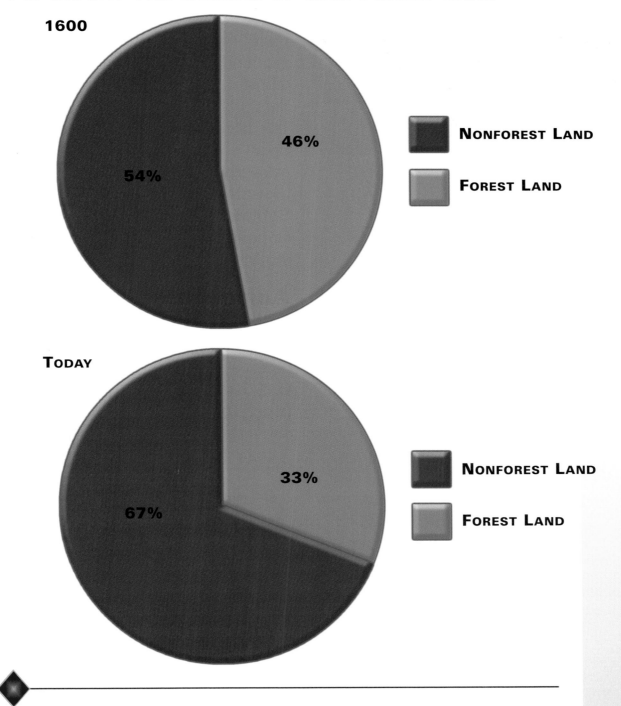

1600

54%

46%

◼ NONFOREST LAND

◼ FOREST LAND

TODAY

67%

33%

◼ NONFOREST LAND

◼ FOREST LAND

Pie charts are great for showing percentage or proportional distribution. Even if the actual percentages were not provided, these charts clearly show a dramatic shift in proportions of forest to nonforest lands in the United States between 1600 and today.

A woman works on a rice paddy in Kengha, Vietnam, for which rice is an important export crop. Wet rice farming is a major source of methane gas.

past few centuries has vastly reduced the number of frontier lands in the world. Today's frontiers lie primarily in rain forests. The lowland rain forests of Brazil's Amazon River basin have attracted settlers from more mountainous regions. Likewise, Southeast Asia's rain forests and Nepal's lowland Terai zone have attracted many settlers.

AGRICULTURE

Somewhere between a quarter and a fifth of Earth's total land surface is suitable for agriculture. Only half that amount is currently used. The land cover for nearly all of today's farmland has been converted from forest, grassland, marshland, or even desert. The remaining potential farmland is of relatively poor quality.

The least intensive method of land conversion is slash-and-burn agriculture, in which ground cover is cut and burned to provide nutrients to poor soil. The plot is productive for five or six growing seasons. The farmer then moves on to another plot of land while allowing the ground cover on the old plot to reestablish itself, a process that takes several years. At this point, it will be burned and planted into crops again.

Wet rice farming is the most labor-intensive form of agricultural conversion. In wet rice farming, lowlands are flooded and partitioned into paddies. Before planting, the farmer must construct embankments and channel water to fill the paddy. The paddies have to be cleaned periodically, while the embankments and water channels need frequent care.

Generally, farmers in industrialized countries raise the one crop that grows best in their particular region. Synthetic fertilizers increase crop yields, pesticides protect crops from harmful insects, and irrigation keeps the plants healthy while allowing the farmer to work in areas that would otherwise be too arid.

Grassland, often used as rangeland for grazing livestock, makes up about a quarter of Earth's land surface. This figure has remained virtually unchanged since 1700. Two human activities tend to keep this number constant. The expansion of urban areas and settlements, as well as the expansion of croplands through irrigation, reduces natural grasslands. At the same time, tropical forests and other areas are cleared, opening up new rangeland.

While the amount of grassland has remained stable, the world's increasing human population and demand for meat have led to an increase in the number of animals grazing on marginal

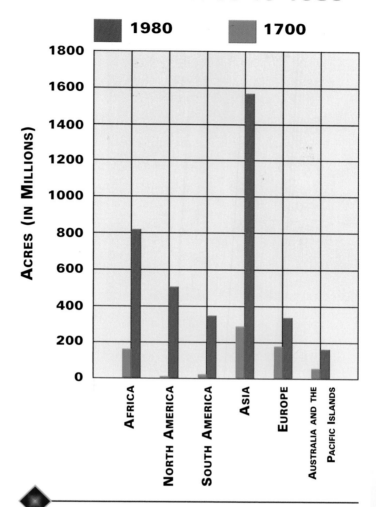

Bar charts are useful for making quantitative comparisons between two or more things. This bar chart presents the increase in cropland on six continents between 1700 and 1980.

A house collapses during a mudslide in Forest Falls, California, on July 11, 1999. Significantly reducing the number of trees in hilly regions increases the risk of mudslides and other forms of mass wasting.

rangeland. As this land receives more use, the sparse vegetation is further reduced. This can lead to a process called desertification. Desertification occurs when animals overgraze grasslands, eating the plants that hold the soil in place. Animals also damage the soil by compacting it with their hooves, making it more difficult for new plants to grow in the area. When combined with a climatic change such as a drought, the topsoil is blown away and the area is left barren.

Wetlands and Forests

About 3.3 million square miles (8.5 million square kilometers) of Earth's surface are made up of various types of wetlands. An estimated 5.8 million square miles (15 million sq km) have been drained or filled in, mostly during the past century. Wetlands have long been considered unproductive and useless territory, and their conversion to dry land viewed in only a positive light.

Today, however, the benefits of pristine wetlands are widely recognized. Swamps and other inland wetlands provide habitats for fish and waterfowl, absorb pollution, and retain water that would otherwise flood nearby regions. The advantages of draining wetlands for agriculture are often short-lived, as the soil quickly deteriorates. Coastal wetlands such as tidal flats, mangrove swamps, and salt marshes are also threatened by conversion to urban areas. Coastal wetlands are drained or filled to make more space for commercial ports or settlements. Like inland wetlands, these regions become vulnerable to soil degradation and flooding.

Unlike that of wetlands, the value of forests has long been appreciated by humans. Current estimates state that forests cover about three times the land area of cropland. Forests provide wood for human uses, protect the soil and the flow of water, and play a part in regulating local climates. However, forests are sometimes considered an obstacle to agricultural expansion and the construction of settlements. They are cleared not only for the timber, but also to create space for the expansion of human enterprise. Wooded plots are cut down along timbering frontiers for lumber and pulp. Woodlands near agricultural settlements are cleared to open more land for cultivation. Near large urban areas, forests are thinned for firewood.

Scientists estimate that the world's forested

SEQUENCE CHART: HOW DESERTIFICATION OCCURS

LIVESTOCK GRAZE ON MARGINAL RANGELAND.

NATIVE GRASSES DIE OUT DUE TO OVERGRAZING.

THE SOIL IS COMPACTED BY THE LIVESTOCK, MAKING IT HARDER FOR NEW GRASSES TO GROW.

THE GROUND COVER BECOMES SPARSE.

TOPSOIL IS EXPOSED AND DRIES OUT DURING A DROUGHT.

HIGH WINDS BLOW THE TOPSOIL AWAY, LEAVING A DESERT BEHIND.

Sequence charts are useful for illustrating the major steps of a process or event. This sequence chart shows the progression of events leading to desertification.

area is about 3.1 million square miles (8 million sq km) smaller than it was 10,000 years ago. About 20 percent of that clearance took place before 1650, while about 30 percent occurred in the 200 years between 1650 and 1850. That means about 1.5 million square miles (4 million sq km) of forest have been cleared since 1850.

Although forests are considered a renewable resource, they can be depleted by aggressive removal and take decades to

CLUSTER CHART: TYPES OF WETLANDS

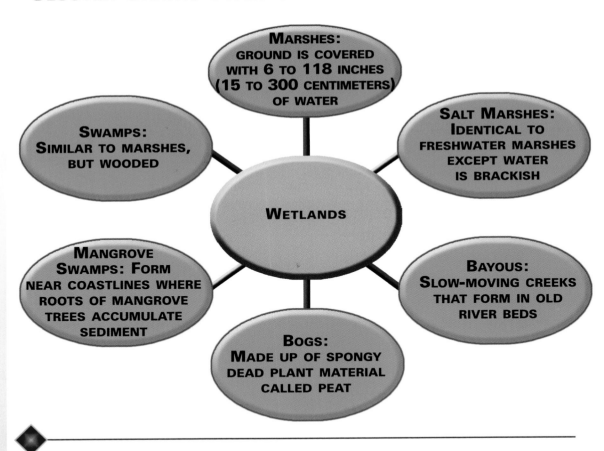

This cluster chart lists and explains the defining features of the six types of wetlands.

recover. In some parts of the world, forests are regenerating on abandoned timbering frontiers and unused farmland. Forests are being depleted rapidly, however, in the developing world, where many landowners have their woodlands cut down for crops, livestock, or timber to meet the demands of a rapidly growing world population.

Soil erosion often results when woodlands have been cleared from hilly or mountainous regions. Tree roots hold topsoil in place. When the trees are removed, nothing remains to keep the soil from washing away. This eventually leads to a condition called mass wasting, in which soil and rock slide downslope, leaving a muddy, barren wasteland behind. The loss of habitat brought by removal of forests threatens animal species, while a reduced number of trees contribute, to an increase of carbon dioxide in the atmosphere.

THE HUMAN FOOTPRINT ON THE LAND

Urban growth and suburban sprawl swallow up grasslands, forests, and wetlands, but the human impact in settled areas extends further than the clearing of land. Industrialization, mass production, and the human quest for convenience make a wide variety of synthetic chemicals available to the average consumer. Goods such as paints, cleaners, and cosmetics, and petroleum products such as gasoline often end up in the soil. There they can damage the soil's quality, or bond with nutrients taken in by plants, which are later consumed by people.

Another consequence of modern life and population growth is the ever-increasing production of garbage. Household trash is usually disposed of in landfills, where it is buried under mounds of soil. Industry produces huge amounts of toxic waste. Nuclear waste from power plants is extremely dangerous and difficult to dispose of safely. Disposal sites for any type of waste must be located away from human settlements so that the waste will not contaminate water supplies.

Containers dump garbage at a landfill in Mountain View, California. As it decomposes, the garbage in landfills emits methane gas for up to thirty years. In recent years, some U.S. landfills have been converting the methane gas into a clean energy source.

The human quest for resources has brought people to remote areas. Mines in deserts, mountains, and foothills can cause permanent damage to fragile local ecosystems. Drilling for oil occurs in environments ranging from swamps to deserts and can severely contaminate nearby soil.

CHAPTER THREE
THE EARTH'S WATER

On its purest form, water is a colorless, odorless, tasteless substance. It is the most universal known solvent, vital to the survival of all known forms of life. It is also one of the most versatile substances on Earth, commonly found in solid, liquid, and gaseous forms. It exists in precipitation, polar ice caps, bodies of water such as oceans and streams, glaciers, and clouds.

Water is perpetually changing forms on Earth through a process called the water cycle. During the water cycle, water falls from the atmosphere to Earth's surface as precipitation, usually in the form of rain. On the surface, the ground absorbs some water while the rest either flows to existing bodies of water or evaporates back into the atmosphere as water vapor, eventually cooling and returning to Earth as precipitation.

THE WORLD'S FRESHWATER

The oceans contain most of Earth's water, but most life-forms that live on land could not exist without freshwater, free of ocean salt. Although we usually associate freshwater with lakes and streams, the largest portion of the world's freshwater supply is frozen in glaciers and polar ice. About 2 million cubic miles (8.2 million cubic kilometers) is stored underground in sediment and bedrock, while inland seas and soil hold only about 72,000 to 96,000 cubic miles (300,000 to 400,000 cu km) of water. Some water also exists in the atmosphere and in the tissues of plants and animals.

Water is a plentiful resource, but it is unevenly distributed throughout the world. Even locations that frequently

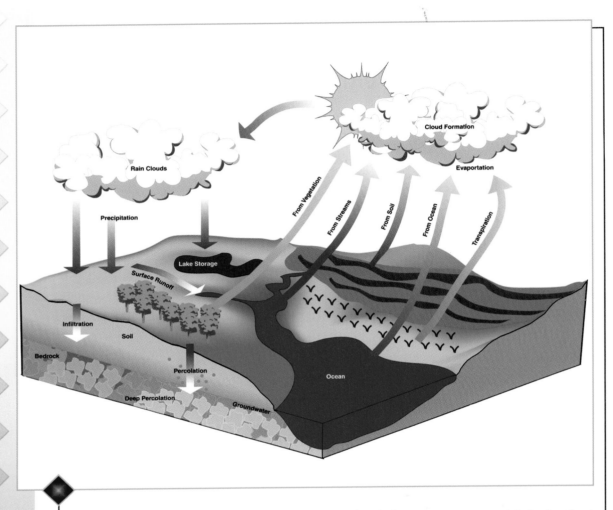

This diagram illustrates the water cycle. It has arrows and labels that shows the direction that the various water forms travel in each stage of the cycle.

experience high annual or long-term rainfall averages go through periods of seasonal shortfalls or droughts. Areas where monsoons are common, for example, are considered well-watered because of the rainy season. Yet they typically experience a dry season during which they get only scant amounts of precipitation. Even in well-watered regions, high demand can affect water supplies.

Reservoirs of surface water are constantly changing and shaping the land. Rivers may shift their courses. Sea levels fluctuate over time. These natural changes can help scientists determine the impact of human use on water levels in reservoirs of surface water.

Groundwater flows underground in vast networks of permeable material called aquifers. It naturally rises to the surface where it seeps from springs, or it is pumped from the ground through wells and renewed as precipitation seeps through the soil. In many dry areas, aquifers are being overdrawn for agriculture and human consumption. Water levels in some parts of the massive Ogallala Aquifer, which lies under portions of eight states from South Dakota to Texas, have dropped off hundreds of feet.

Surface water levels have also dropped as use has increased. In recent years, for example, the water levels of the Caspian and Aral seas have fallen drastically as a result of both increased human usage and drought. These water-level drops worry residents, but on a geologic scale they are dwarfed by earlier decreases. Nonetheless, the current drop in water level in these two seas has occurred far more rapidly than on previous occasions.

EXPLODING PIE CHART: FRESHWATER SUPPLIES ON EARTH

1%
23%
76%
POLAR ICE AND GLACIERS
GROUNDWATER
OTHER (LAND SURFACE SOURCES, THE ATMOSPHERE, PLANTS AND ANIMALS)

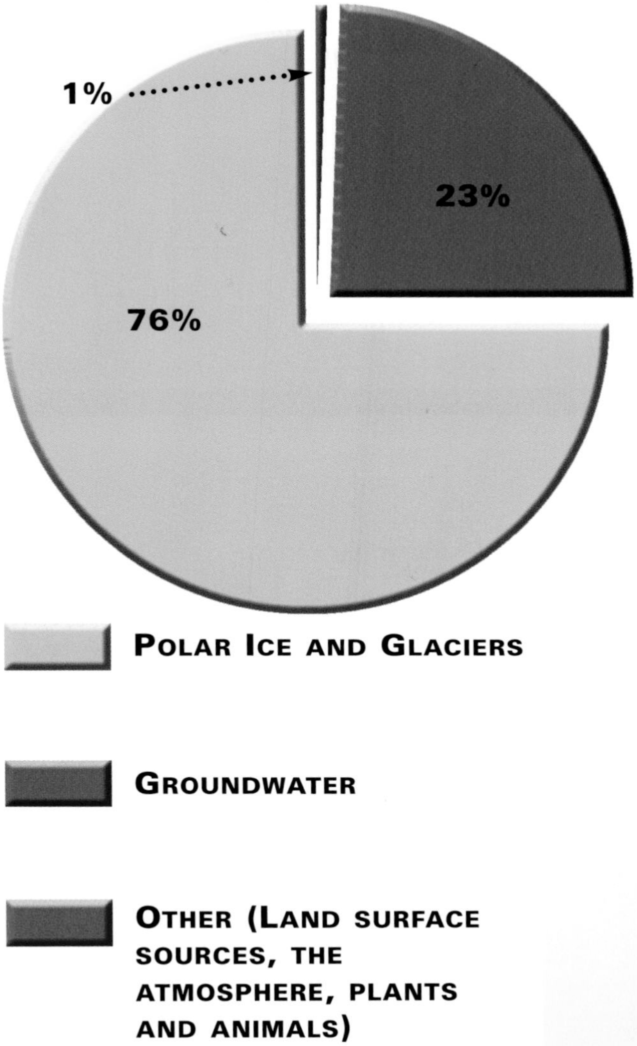

This pie chart shows where the world's freshwater supplies are found.

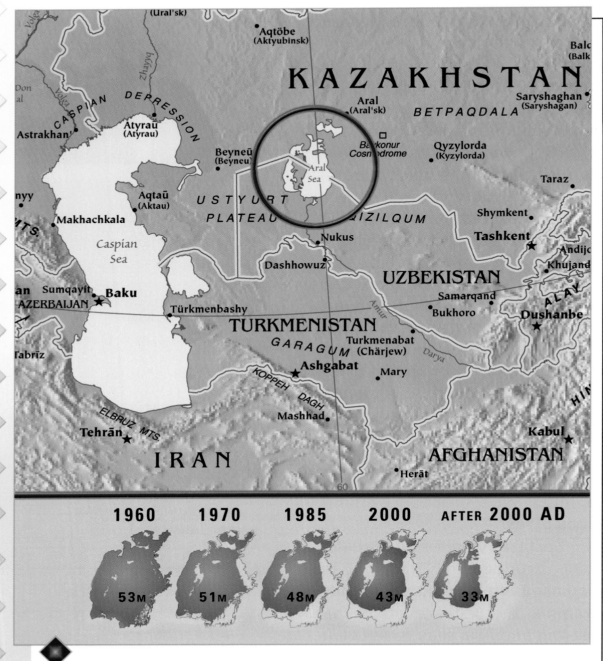

Maps are illustrations that show locations. Some are detailed, showing borders, cities, mountains, and water bodies. Others are basic outlines of the shape of a region. The top map shows the location of the Aral Sea in Central Asia, and the sequence of maps below shows the receding borders since 1960.

TRANSPORTING WATER

Humans need water for drinking and hygiene, to grow crops, and for industrial production. Because of problems of climate, expense, and geography, it is difficult for people to increase local water supplies by drawing on new sources. Polar ice and groundwater are generally difficult to access and are unavailable for use. Much of the world's water supply is drawn from freshwater lakes, streams, and ponds. Modern rearrangements of tanks, reservoirs, pipes, and filters have helped people move water more efficiently. This increased ease of water transfer has allowed settlement in areas once too dry for human habitation. Still, even modern methods of distributing water are limited. Aqueducts, channels, and pipelines can only bring so much water to an area, prohibiting growth in the region beyond a certain point. Therefore, arid regions remain sparsely populated areas.

People increase the amount of available water by expanding the total volume of water in the area. Civic projects, such as pipelines and dams, transport and store water. Existing supplies can be purified in such a way as to make them drinkable through processes such as desalination or chlorination.

The majority of freshwater taken from the water cycle is used for agricultural irrigation. Irrigation drains and depletes surface water supplies in streams. Most of this water is consumed by plants, or evaporates into the air and is not returned to the streams. Ultimately, this results in lower water levels for lakes and seas such as the Aral, as the streams that supply them carry less water. Runoff from irrigated fields introduces contaminants such as pesticides, salt, and fertilizers into streams. Topsoil and silt runoff from recently cleared lands build up in streams, depriving the water of oxygen and decreasing flow.

POLLUTION

Industrial complexes and factories have long used water as a means of disposing waste and generating steam and electricity.

This is an aerial view of Hoover Dam, one of the largest dams in the world. Completed in 1936, it is a primary source of electrical power and flood control in the American Southwest.

Industrial usage often introduces waste products into streams, which is eventually carried off to lakes and seas. Most of the water used in industry functions as a coolant and is then returned to the body of water from which it was taken. Excess heat from cooling tanks is the primary waste product generated by industry. The heated water cools rapidly when returned to its source, but often leaves water temperatures immediately downstream too warm for ecosystems to survive.

Toxic substances released into the water by industrial facilities can pose a great threat to plants, animals, and humans. Many industrial pollutants, such as mercury, are incredibly harmful. Groundwater contamination from chemical runoff is particularly troubling because it takes a very long time for underground supplies to be rid of chemicals.

Water usage in human settlements mirrors agricultural usage in many ways. Water is usually taken from a surface supply and distributed to urban consumers. The water returned to the supply is usually contaminated with sewage, chemicals, salt, detergents, and other waste.

HUMAN IMPACT ON THE OCEANS

Humans have had a relatively smaller impact on the world's vast ocean system than on freshwater supplies. The greatest problems facing the oceans are pollution and overfishing. People have dumped garbage directly into the oceans for centuries, typically near shores. This dumping harms human interests by clogging shipping lanes, disrupting ocean habitats, and causing bacterial outbreaks in coastal cities and towns.

Chemical pollutants are damaging to oceans and ocean life. The effect of pesticides, herbicides, and fertilizers is the most easily observed. In some areas, the concentrations of such chemicals are high enough to create lifeless zones in the oceans, particularly close to land. Shellfish and coral reef environments are especially vulnerable to these pollutants. Heavy metals, such as lead and mercury, flow into oceans from factories and eventually end up in the food chain. There, they are eaten by fish and shellfish, which are later caught and consumed by humans.

FLOW CHART: CHEMICAL RUNOFF IN A FIELD

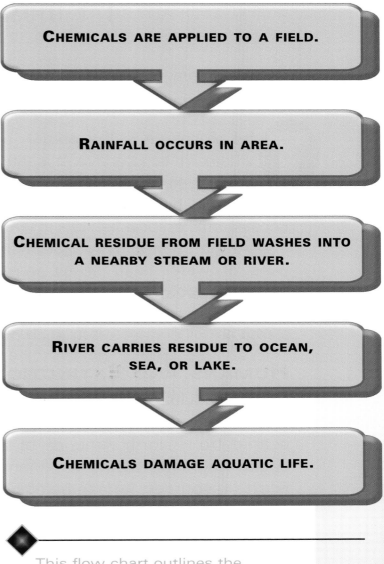

This flow chart outlines the stages and consequences of chemical runoff.

CHAPTER FOUR

THE BIOSPHERE

The biosphere is the portion of Earth's air, land, and water where life can survive. It is the global ecological system integrating all living things and their interactions with other species and the elements. The biosphere is further divided into ecosystems, or local habitats in which organisms live and interact.

Any human activity that changes the quality of local supplies of water, soil, or air impacts the life-forms within a particular ecosystem. Changes in the population of one species within the ecosystem often affect other species, since its life-forms are all connected to each other by their interactions.

HUMANS AND EXTINCTION

Human activity may have caused extinctions 10,000 years ago, when large mammals such as the woolly mammoth disappeared from North America at the same time that humans began migrating to the continent in large numbers. In using Earth's resources, human beings have often ignored the needs of Earth's other inhabitants. Some species have become extinct, while many others have been reduced in population to the point that they are endangered. Though these changes began taking place at the dawn of civilization, they have recently accelerated at a frightening pace.

Estimating the scale at which humans have caused extinctions is difficult because the total number of species of life on Earth is unknown. A million and a half species have been classified, but more are discovered every day. The discovery of new species of

TIMELINE: RECENT SPECIES EXTINCTIONS CAUSED BY HUMANS

1500	THE MOA IS HUNTED TO EXTINCTION IN NEW ZEALAND.
1850	THE GREAT AUK IS HUNTED TO EXTINCTION.
1875	THE LAST TARPAN DIES IN A MOSCOW ZOO.
1883	THE QUAGGA IS HUNTED TO EXTINCTION IN AFRICA.
1911	THE PASSENGER PIGEON IS HUNTED TO EXTINCTION IN NORTH AMERICA.
1936	THE TASMANIAN WOLF BECOMES EXTINCT IN AUSTRALIA.
1989	THE GOLDEN TOAD IS DECLARED EXTINCT.
2000	THE RED COLOBUS MONKEY IS DECLARED EXTINCT.

A timeline is useful for listing events in chronological order. The events do not need to be related. This timeline provides a list of species extinctions, dating back to 1500, attributed to human activities.

plants and animals is also expanding earlier notions of species diversity. New species are often discovered as human populations push into new frontiers, meaning that their habitats are endangered virtually the moment they are discovered.

The recent loss of species diversity is closely linked to human activity. Habitat changes by humans, no matter how small, can have an enormous impact on animal populations. For example, grizzly bears once ranged over most of the Pacific Northwest. Due to deforestation of their territory and overhunting, the population of grizzly bears in the United States has fallen to the point that the species is listed as threatened.

The disappearance of one species from an ecosystem can have drastic consequences for other species. The flightless dodo bird was hunted to extinction in Mauritius around 1693. Although it is one of the most famous cases of extinction brought by humans, few people know that it threatens the tambalacoque tree. The fruit-eating dodo prepared the tree's seeds for germination in its gizzard before they passed out of the bird's body. Without the dodo, the tambalacoque tree has not been able to reproduce in 300 years. Today, only six tambalacoque trees remain.

IDEA RAKE: FACTORS AFFECTING PLANT DIVERSITY

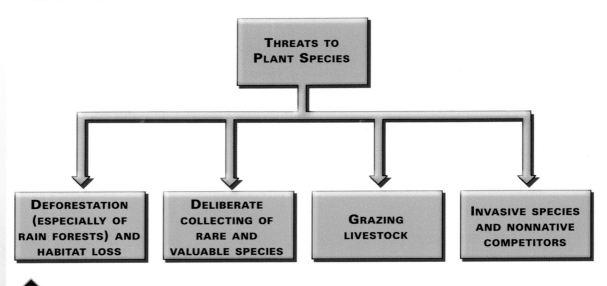

An idea rake is a simple tree diagram in the shape of a rake that shows supporting details for a main concept. This idea rake shows four factors that affect plant diversity.

INTRODUCED SPECIES

Humans sometimes disrupt species populations by introducing new species into habitats. Many introduced species can coexist with native species. A small minority, however, can cause major problems for native species. Ordinarily, species populations are kept in balance by interactions with other species. Each species fills a niche as defined by the way that it uses the habitat's resources. Some species throw these balances off as they are introduced to habitats with no natural enemies to limit their population growth.

These invasive species fall into several categories. Animals are sometimes intentionally introduced to a habitat for hunting. In Australia, introduced rabbits have severely damaged crops and grasslands. Nonnative plants introduced to prevent erosion or for ornamentation can outcompete native grasses and shrubs. Kudzu, for example, was planted throughout the American South during the 1930s to prevent soil erosion. Today, the hardy kudzu has overrun many parts of the South. Many insect species are unintentionally introduced, and can cause severe damage to local crops and trees. The emerald ash borer entered the United States at some point during the late 1980s by stowing away in shipping crates or infested lumber from Asia. Since then, they have been killing ash trees throughout the Great Lakes region.

AQUATIC LIFE

Human activity has reduced population sizes and the diversity of aquatic life across the world. Overfishing is the most pressing threat in the oceans, while freshwater species also face pollution, habitat loss, and competition from invasive species.

Dams constructed to provide water for towns and farms negatively affect river life by changing river currents and water levels. Some fish, such as trout, are best suited for fast-moving streams with oxygen-rich water. Dams slow the downstream currents and

INVASIVE SPECIES	AREA INTRODUCED	YEAR	IMPACT ON NATIVE SPECIES
SEA LAMPREY	GREAT LAKES	1959	OUTCOMPETES LAKE TROUT
RABBIT	AUSTRALIA	1859	DAMAGES NATIVE PLANTS, IMPACTING OTHER SMALL MAMMALS
BROWN TREE SNAKE	GUAM	1945	DECIMATES LOCAL BIRDS AND FRUIT BATS
KUDZU	U.S.	1876	CROWDS OUT OTHER GROUND PLANTS AND SHRUBS
FIRE ANTS	U.S.	1930s	DRIVES OUT OTHER ANT AND SMALL ANIMAL SPECIES
AXIS DEER	HAWAII	1959	OVERGRAZES NATIVE PLANTS

This graphic organizer is a four-column chart, which can be used to illustrate all kinds of facts. This chart gives examples of nonnative species that were introduced into the United States, and the resulting effects on the environment. It also tells the years and the regions in which the new species were introduced.

lower the downstream water level. The fish downstream must survive with less water than in their natural habitat.

As on land, invasive species enter freshwater habitats and disrupt local ecosystems. Some fish have been intentionally released into freshwater systems. The Nile perch was introduced into Africa's Lake Victoria during the 1950s. It outcompeted local fish species, driving many to extinction. Some fish or amphibians are bought as pets and released into the wild, such as the predatory northern snakehead, a fish species native to China and Korea that had been sold in U.S. pet stores. Since the first introduced snakehead was found in a Maryland pond in 2002, the fish has been spotted in waterways in twelve other states. Others are accidentally introduced to their new environments. The zebra mussel, for example, entered the Great Lakes in the ballast water of foreign ships at some point during the late 1980s. Since then, they have sent many freshwater shellfish species native to the Great Lakes into decline by outcompeting them for resources.

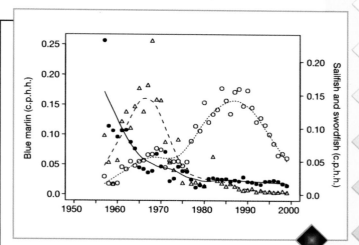

Overfishing eventually leads to a drop in the species population. This line graph shows the catch per 100 hooks of blue marlins (solid circles, solid lines), sailfish (open triangle, dashed line), and swordfish (open circles, dotted line) between 1950 and 2000.

Humans have become incredibly efficient at capturing fish by using huge nets to troll through the oceans. These fishing practices have significantly reduced the populations of many species of fish. Shellfish living near shores are threatened both by overharvesting and by pollution. Coral reefs, which provide habitats for a wide variety of ocean life, are particularly sensitive to environmental changes such as warmer temperatures and pollution. Marine mammals, such as otters and seals, have been threatened by hunters seeking their prized fur.

Whales are one of the most dramatic examples representing the dangers humans represent to other life-forms. The nineteenth-century whaling industry pursued many whale species to the brink of extinction. Though most species of whales have not been actively hunted in decades, many species populations remain at only a fraction of what they once were.

CHAPTER FIVE

THE FUTURE OF THE EARTH

Humans have dramatically changed the world since the beginning of the Industrial Revolution. Few of these changes have been positive for the environment and other species. The human race depends on natural resources for its well-being. Ecosystems provide people with food, water, and the raw materials for shelter and comfort. As the growing world population requires more natural resources, people have cleared forests, drained swamps, dammed rivers, and pushed out other species, sometimes causing extinctions.

In 2001, the United Nations launched a broad study of the global ecosystem. The Millennium Ecosystem Assessment (MA) included more than 1,300 scientists from all over the world. The MA's conclusions, which became public in 2005, demonstrate not only how human activity affects Earth, but also how humans themselves are affected.

The MA's report found that human beings have had a greater impact on ecosystems since 1950 than at any other point in history. Most of these changes have come as humans sought food, fuel, freshwater, timber, and fibers. These changes have led to major gains in human well-being and economic development for portions of the world's population, but have come at a cost to Earth's future. The ecological problems caused by human activities have led to a sizable and largely irreversible loss of species diversity. Earth's natural resources are being depleted by misuse. If this trend continues, future generations will not be able to benefit from the use of these same resources.

SPIDER MAP: CONSEQUENCES OF RISING OCEAN LEVELS

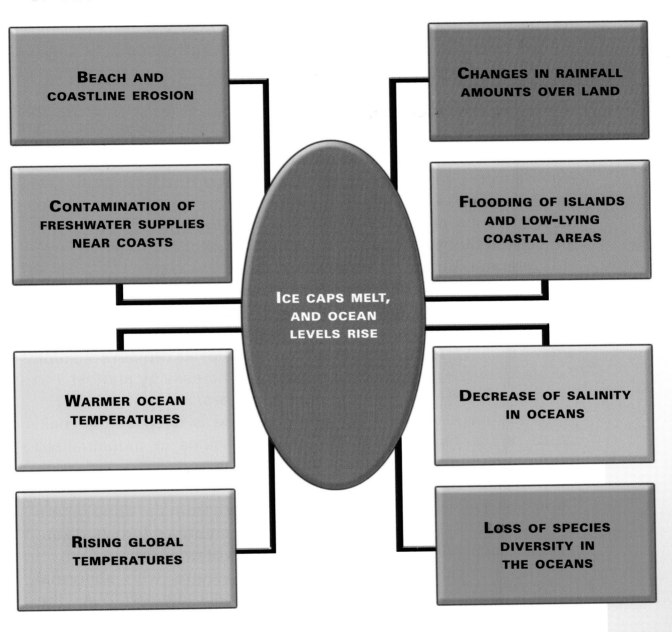

BEACH AND COASTLINE EROSION

CHANGES IN RAINFALL AMOUNTS OVER LAND

CONTAMINATION OF FRESHWATER SUPPLIES NEAR COASTS

FLOODING OF ISLANDS AND LOW-LYING COASTAL AREAS

ICE CAPS MELT, AND OCEAN LEVELS RISE

WARMER OCEAN TEMPERATURES

DECREASE OF SALINITY IN OCEANS

RISING GLOBAL TEMPERATURES

LOSS OF SPECIES DIVERSITY IN THE OCEANS

A spider chart can be a fun way to illustrate supporting details of a concept. It is basically a cluster chart in the shape of a spider. This chart gives eight effects of a rise in ocean levels.

Atmospheric changes brought on by global warming may currently pose the greatest threat to life on Earth. The melting of glaciers and polar ice threatens to raise ocean levels. Warmer oceans could significantly alter global weather patterns, changes that would damage ecosystems worldwide.

THE CHANGING WEATHER

The world's climate has fluctuated throughout Earth's history. Earth was far warmer during the time of the dinosaurs, and has experienced periodic ice ages during which much of its surface has been frozen. Scientists disagree on the causes of most of these historical climate changes. However, there is little doubt that the current global warming pattern is the result of human activity.

Average global temperatures have increased by 1 to 2 degrees Fahrenheit (0.6 degrees Celsius) since 1856. The rate of change accelerated after World War II. This temperature increase is usually attributed to an increase in greenhouse gases. Studies predict that even if current greenhouse gas levels remain constant, the global average temperatures may still increase by another 1 to 2 degrees Fahrenheit over the next 100 years.

The recent increase of carbon dioxide is cited as the main cause of the temperature increase. Emissions in industrialized nations such as the United States, combined with worldwide deforestation, contribute heavily to the increase of carbon dioxide. Forests also affect rainfall, retaining moisture from the atmosphere so that it cycles back to the forest. When an area's forests disappear, the local climate becomes noticeably drier.

The warming oceans threaten ecosystems with abnormal weather patterns. Precipitation is generally created over the oceans and other large bodies of water when water temperatures and air temperatures collide to form weather fronts. Fronts close to shore often move over land, bringing precipitation.

As global warming brings warmer temperatures to some areas, others grow unexpectedly cooler. Areas that once received ample

DESCRIBING WHEEL: POSSIBLE CLIMATIC EFFECTS OF GLOBAL WARMING

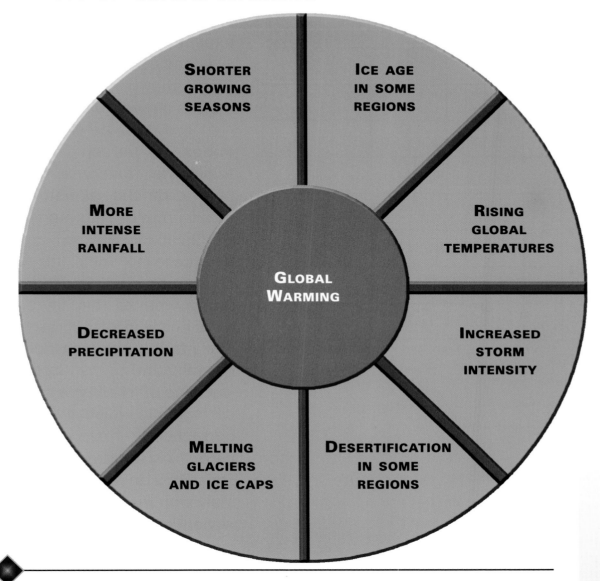

A describing wheel is a chart that is typically used to list the characteristics of something. This describing wheel outlines some climatic consequences of global warming.

rain now receive too little, leading to droughts and fires, while normally dry regions experience abnormal rainy seasons. Changes in ocean currents in the South and Central Pacific have introduced the El Niño and La Niña weather patterns. Many scientists speculate that the intense hurricanes that have battered North and Central

LINE GRAPH: WORLD POPULATION CHANGE SINCE 1700

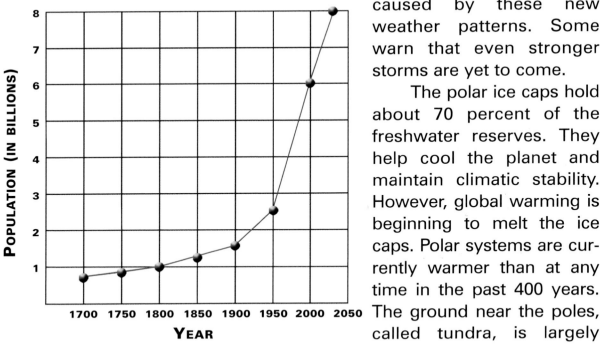

DATA

1700 — 700 MILLION

1750 — 900 MILLION

1800 — 1 BILLION

1850 — 1.2 BILLION

1900 — 1.6 BILLION

1950 — 2.5 BILLION

2000 — 6 BILLION

2027 — 8 BILLION

Line graphs are useful for showing trends. This graph shows the rise in human population between 1700 and 2000, and projects what it will be in 2027.

America in recent years are caused by these new weather patterns. Some warn that even stronger storms are yet to come.

The polar ice caps hold about 70 percent of the freshwater reserves. They help cool the planet and maintain climatic stability. However, global warming is beginning to melt the ice caps. Polar systems are currently warmer than at any time in the past 400 years. The ground near the poles, called tundra, is largely made up of a soil type called permafrost, which contains permanently frozen water. Permafrost tundra in northern Russia and Canada makes up the world's largest wetlands. With global warming, the permafrost melts during the region's short growing season rather than remaining solidly frozen. The layer close to the surface of the ground thaws during the warm season. In recent years, there have been record amounts of melting, which is attributed to global warming. Large-scale melting could release significant amounts of carbon dioxide, which could affect the local ecosystem.

As ice caps melt, the water trapped within them reaches the ocean. Thus, the water levels of the world's oceans are gradually rising. Rising ocean levels flood coastal lowlands, threatening humans and other species living in those areas. The process also converts the freshwater that had been frozen into salty ocean water, removing it from Earth's freshwater reserves.

The general warming of the atmosphere also impacts the water cycle. Warmer atmospheric temperatures prevent some water vapor from reentering the water cycle as precipitation. The suspended water vapor further affects the climate by adding to greenhouse gases in the atmosphere. Reduced precipitation and depleted water supplies increase the frequency and severity of droughts. Droughts combine with overgrazing of grassland and deforestation to speed the process of desertification. Desertification is occurring most rapidly in parts of Asia, where tropical forests have been cut to create new rangeland for livestock.

THE HUMAN THREAT

Humans have directly or indirectly contributed to many of the problems facing the world's ecosystems and their future. Many of these changes are the result of human industry and misuse of the environment. Much of this misuse occurred as the human population grew dramatically following the beginning of the Industrial Revolution. Innovations in agriculture and technology enabled people to produce more food than ever before and to move into regions that had been sparsely settled. These human advances helped foster a period of enormous human population growth that continues today. Since 1961, the world's population has doubled, from 3 billion people to more than 6 billion. Estimates for future population growth predict that there will be 8 billion people on Earth by the year 2027.

As the world's population continues to grow, so does the strain upon Earth's resources. The degradation of Earth's ecosystems is

DONUT CHART: ENERGY USE WORLDWIDE

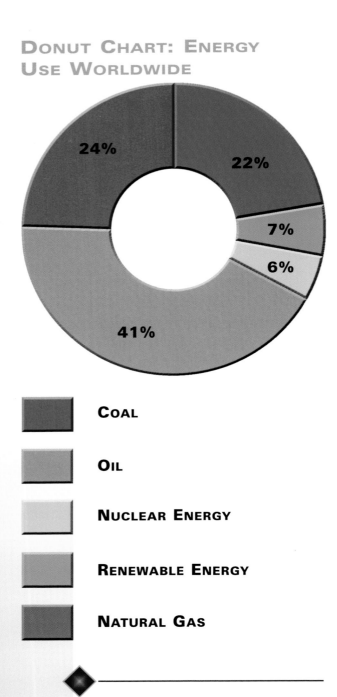

- **COAL**
- **OIL**
- **NUCLEAR ENERGY**
- **RENEWABLE ENERGY**
- **NATURAL GAS**

The donut chart is a variation of the pie chart. This donut chart measures the use of five types of energy as a percentage of the total global energy consumed.

expected to accelerate over the next fifty years if misuse continues. Many of the same problems, such as deforestation, desertification, and pollution, will continue on a broader scale as populations and industries continue to grow in developing nations.

There are steps that can be taken to slow or even reverse environmental degradation over the next fifty years. Governments and international organizations must encourage citizens and businesses to conserve the world's resources. The use of carbon-producing fossil fuels to generate energy must eventually be phased out in favor of more sustainable energy sources, such as solar, wind, and water power, or hydroelectricity. Landowners must be encouraged to manage their property in ways that protect and enhance ecosystem services such as forests and freshwater supplies. Farms and factories must begin looking for ways to be productive without harming the environment. Exploitation of ocean resources and freshwater supplies must be managed responsibly. Unless these changes take place soon, Earth's growing human population faces an uncertain future.

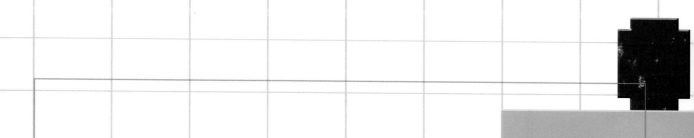

GLOSSARY

absorption band A dark band in the spectrum of white light transmitted through some material. The pattern of the lines can be used to identify the material.

chlorination The disinfection of water by adding small amounts of chlorine or chlorine compounds.

desalination The removal of salt from water in order to make it drinkable.

erosion The wearing down of Earth's surface.

monsoon A wind system that changes direction with the seasons.

organism An individual life-form.

ozone A poisonous form of oxygen, O_3. It is a pollutant in the lower atmosphere, but it forms a layer in the upper atmosphere that acts as a screen for ultraviolet radiation.

solvent A substance in which another substance, the solute, is dissolved.

species Populations of organisms capable of breeding and producing offspring.

spectrum The array of color produced by the dispersal of light, arranged in order of wavelengths.

stratosphere The layer of the atmosphere 10 to 30 miles (16 to 48 km) above Earth's surface.

troposphere The lowest level of the atmosphere, found between Earth's surface and the stratosphere.

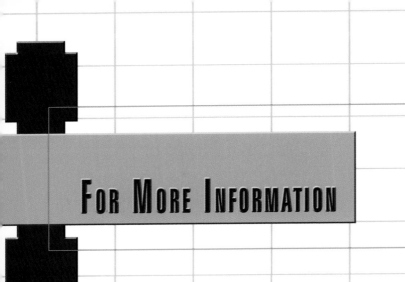

For More Information

Environmental Protection Agency
Ariel Rios Building
1200 Pennsylvania Avenue, NW
Washington, DC 20460
(202) 272-0167
Web site: http://www.epa.gov

National Wildlife Federation
11100 Wildlife Center Drive
Reston, VA 20190-5362
(800) 822-9919
Web site: http://www.nwf.org

U.S. Fish and Wildlife Service
The Endangered Species Program
4401 N. Fairfax Drive, Room 420
Arlington, VA 22203
Web site: http://endangered.fws.gov

WEB SITES

Due to the changing nature of Internet links, the Rosen Publishing Group, Inc., has developed an online list of Web sites related to the subject of this book. This site is updated regularly. Please use this link to access the list:

http://www.rosenlinks.com/ugosle/higo

FOR FURTHER READING

Mackay, Richard. *The Penguin Atlas of Endangered Species*. New York, NY: Penguin Books, 2002.

Martin, Patricia A. Fink. *Rivers and Streams*. New York, NY: Franklin Watts, 1999.

Morgan, Sally. *Ecology and Environment: The Cycles of Life*. New York, NY: Oxford University Press, 1995.

Patent, Dorothy Hinshaw. *Biodiversity*. New York, NY: Clarion Books, 1996.

Pollock, Steve. *Ecology*. New York, NY: Dorling Kindersley, 1993.

Pringle, Laurence. *The Environmental Movement: From Its Roots to the Challenges of a New Century*. New York, NY: Harper Collins Publishers, 2000.

BIBLIOGRAPHY

Appenzeller, Tim, et al. "The Heat Is On." *National Geographic*, Vol. 206, No. 3, pp. 2–75.

Goudie, Andrew. *The Human Impact on the Natural Environment*, 5th ed. Cambridge, MA: MIT Press, 2000.

McGrath, Susan. "Alien Invaders." *National Geographic*, Vol. 207, No. 3, pp. 92–117.

Meyer, William B. *Human Impact on the Earth*. New York, NY: Cambridge University Press, 1996.

Silver, Cheryl Simon, and Ruth S. Defries. *One Earth, One Future: Our Changing Global Environment*. Washington, DC: National Academy Press, 1990.

Slobodkin, Lawrence B. *A Citizens Guide to Ecology*. New York, NY: Oxford University Press, 2003.

Starr, Cecie. *Biology: Concepts and Applications*. Belmont, CA: Wadsworth Publishing Company, 1997.

Tickle, Amy L. *Ecology and the Environment: A Look at Ecosystems of the World*. Ann Arbor, MI: The University of Michigan Press, 1995.

Weiner, Jonathan. *The Next One Hundred Years: Shaping the Fate of Our Living Earth*. New York, NY: Bantam Books, 1990.

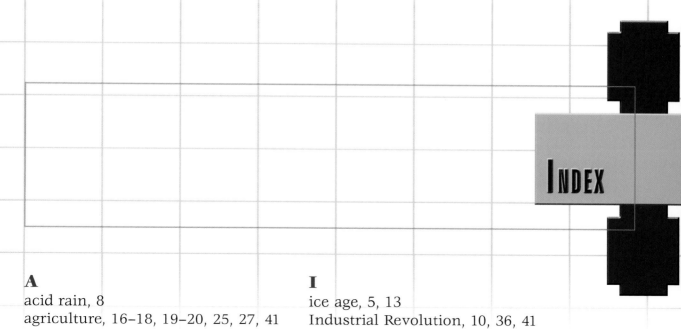

INDEX

ABOUT THE AUTHOR

Jason Porterfield is a writer and researcher who lives in Chicago, Illinois. He has written more than a dozen books on a wide range of subjects. He developed an early interest in environmental issues while growing up in rural Virginia, where he acquired firsthand experience with a great diversity of wildlife. As a child, he was a frequent visitor to the University of Virginia's Biological Station at Mountain Lake.

PHOTO CREDITS

Cover, p. 1, 5 (all three insets boxes) © Royalty-Free/Nova Development Corporation; pp. 4–5 © Corbis; graphics pp. 7, 9, 11, 13, 15, 17, 19, 20, 25, 26, 29, 31, 32, 34, 35, 37, 39, 40, 42 courtesy of Nelson Sá; p. 10 © Bettmann/Corbis; p. 12 © Joseph Sohm/Visions of America/Corbis; p. 16 © Macduff Everton/Corbis; p. 18 © San Bernardino Sun/Corbis; p. 22 © Louie Psihoyos/Corbis; p. 24 © NASA; p. 28 © Lester Lefkowitz/Corbis.

Designer: Nelson Sá; Editor: Wayne Anderson
Photo Researcher: Nelson Sá